THE TRACK THE WHALES MAKE

Ted Kooser Contemporary Poetry

EDITOR
Ted Kooser

THE TRACK
THE WHALES
MAKE New and Selected Poems

MARJORIE SAISER

Introduction by Ted Kooser

University of Nebraska Press LINCOLN

Acknowledgments for the use of copyrighted
material appear on pages xi–xii, which constitute
an extension of the copyright page.

Names: Saiser, Marjorie, author. | Kooser,
Ted, writer of introduction.
Title: The track the whales make: new and selected
poems / Marjorie Saiser; introduction by Ted Kooser.
Description: Lincoln: University of Nebraska Press,
[2021] | Series: Ted Kooser contemporary poetry
Identifiers: LCCN 2021015343
ISBN 9781496228123 (paperback)
ISBN 9781496228888 (epub)
ISBN 9781496228895 (pdf)
Subjects: BISAC: POETRY / Women
Authors | LCGFT: Poetry.
Classification: LCC PS3569.A4543 T73 2021 |
DDC 811/.54—dc23
LC record available at https://lccn.loc.gov/2021015343

Set in Adobe Garamond by Laura Buis.
Designed by N. Putens.

CONTENTS

From *Lost in Seward County*, 2001

From *Bones of a Very Fine Hand*, 1999

ACKNOWLEDGMENTS

Sincere gratitude to the editors of the journals in which some of these poems were first published—*Prairie Schooner, Poetry East, Poet Lore, Nimrod, 1-70 Review, The Fourth River, bosque, burntdistrict, PoetryMagazine.com, Rattle, Water-Stone Review, Crab Orchard Review, Atlanta Review, Cream City Review, The Laurel Review, The Briar Cliff Review,* and *Alaska Quarterly Review*—as well as the editors of the anthologies *Healing the Divide: Poems of Kindness and Connection* (Brattleboro VT: Green Writers Press, 2019) and *Poetry of Presence: An Anthology of Mindfulness Poems* (West Hartford CT: Grayson Books, 2017).

Poems from *Learning to Swim* appear with permission of Stephen F. Austin State University Press (© 2019 by Marjorie Saiser). Poems from *Losing the Ring in the River* appear with permission of the University of New Mexico Press (© 2013 by Marjorie Saiser). Poems from *Bones of a Very Fine Hand* (© 1999 by Marjorie Saiser), *Lost in Seward County* (© 2001 by Marjorie Saiser), *Beside You at the Stoplight* (© 2010 by Marjorie Saiser), *I Have Nothing to Say about Fire* (© 2016 by Marjorie Saiser), and *The Woman in the Moon* (© 2018 by Marjorie Saiser) appear with permission of the Backwaters Press. Very special thanks to the editors of these presses.

"For My Body" is reprinted from *Prairie Schooner* 81, no. 2 (Summer 2007), by permission of the University of Nebraska Press (© 2007 by the University of Nebraska Press). "I Want to Be a Man" is reprinted from *Prairie Schooner* 75, no. 3 (Fall 2001), by permission of the University of Nebraska Press (© 2001 by the University of Nebraska Press). "Mammogram" is reprinted from *Prairie Schooner* 73, no. 2 (Summer 1999), by permission of the University of Nebraska Press (© 1999 by the University of Nebraska Press).

Heartfelt gratitude to those who have nurtured this work, notably: Don Saiser, Hilda Raz, Kimberly Verhines, James Cihlar, Greg Kosmicki, the Prairie Trout, and the Cabin Women.

INTRODUCTION

TED KOOSER

Over many years I've come to believe that it's the personality we readers sense through an author's words that leads us to like a book or not like it.

Once, as an enthusiastic young poet, I sent a poem I was quite proud of to Robert Bly, who by his example was teaching us poets of the middles states how to write about what was at hand. I hadn't yet met Bly but had great admiration for him, as I do today. My poem was about my grandfather's death, about being at his bedside as he died. Robert sent the poem back with a chastening note that said, "You're making this up." How he arrived at that I was never to learn, because I was embarrassed and didn't want to trouble him further, but he must have sensed that there was something not quite true about what I'd written.

All this is to say that an author *shows through*.

You're now holding a book of poems in which the personality is immensely appealing, loveable even. Marjorie Saiser is *right there* in every poem, not up front getting in the way, but just off to the side. Everything about her life is just within reach. She writes what she sees. There's nothing made up about anything here. We don't know that for a fact, but we intuitively *feel* it.

These poems, gathered from her earlier books and with a complement of new work, shine with an attractive personality. We know instinctively that this poet is telling the truth, that she's not making things up. Every poem in this book celebrates a life that is, if seen from a distance, altogether ordinary, quotidian, as she has lived among the rest of us—humble, thankful, generous—a welcome part of our human community. Is there a moment when she sees herself as special? Never. This is one of the most authentic, genuine books you'll ever experience.

As you read through these pages, you'll find this poet present in every room, in every situation, showing herself but not ever so much as to stand in the way. I'm so immensely thankful to the University of Nebraska Press for its trust in my judgment, for indulging me while I introduce you to this poet whom you, too, will love.

THE TRACK THE WHALES MAKE

I Could Taste It

NEW POEMS

The Shirt I Would Have Bought You

The shirt I would have bought you
would have known your shoulders,

the bones of your back.
Settling its weight evenly

it would have longed to touch the
territory, warm and unclaimed beneath it.

With both hands I
yearned to bear down

to rub at the points of the blades
around, around

the thumbs pressing hard, loving
again, again

the fingers making sure of the soft
depths at the base of the neck

the heel of my hand slow
over and over the beauty of it

my face coming close
as if to drink.

Sometimes I Remember to Watch

The sunset in the west is audacious,
but I look east to the mountains
because for a moment they take on
and hold a pinkish glow, borrowed.
Some days I catch it,
I stop doing the Important and Required,
go to a chair on the deck, stay there
for the pink. It's brief, no matter whether
I raise my glass or turn my back.
The glow is, and then is gone
in the time it takes
for one crow to flap across the scene.
Some days I will manage to save.
I toast color. I toast silence
and brevity.

When You Write the Story

Don't leave out the child,
her plump flawless hands,
and the game she invented.

Tell about her face when she hovered
and circled around her father
as he dozed on the carpet and she

placed a stuffed animal
or a puzzle piece on his plaid back,

his neck, his hair, arm, leg.
He was her field.

This is how we see what the world supplies
and move around it, unsteady,

determined to make it ours.

We Wait for the Trogon

we sit on a fallen tree off the trail
nobody else in these woods today
white trunks of sycamores around us
we have been furious with each other again
but putting it away for now not sure why
the climb behind us and this being the grove
where a rare bird has been seen by others
There, you say, and sure enough the trogon
sits on a swaying twig, his green back to us
this is what we wait for, what we've read about
we who have disagreed most disagreeably
about this and that and now comes
a wild contraption we have no control over which—
can you believe it—is flying closer
is choosing a branch in front of our faces
its iridescent head and shoulders its bright eye
will leave us, fly away soon, and what does it matter
this thing with feathers, to have it
upside down on the retina for a brief time
but take my hand, love, and like the mortals we are,
let us see this marvel we have and have not together.

So Bad I Could Taste It

Because the man I was married to
didn't arrive to be with me in the hospital,

the nurse asked (I remember her kindness)
if anyone was coming. I said: *Maybe.*

The next afternoon he came with a small
vase of flowers picked from the neighbor's

rose bush. I knew the neighbor's roses and
knew the vase from my knickknack shelf. This

could be a sweet story, a wonderful story
told and retold as long as we lasted, but we

didn't last. We gave out like old shoes
worn in the rain too many times, stretched,

scratched, dumped into the landfill, the gulls
crying loudly with their flapping.

This was America, land of big dreams,
and he paid a lot of attention to others,

which should be all right, and sometimes it
is. I needed to be loved so much I could

taste it. As we used to say in my hometown:
so much we could taste it. That's what I

wanted. I left him, I came back, I tried,
I don't know what he needed, exactly.

We were together the summer our government
sent a rocket to the moon. The night a human

stepped onto the dust and crust of the moon,
I was watching on television, and I also

stepped out my front door
to see the real thing. I wanted

the luminous coin, big sky over rooftops,
the celestial and the neighborhood.

After a while I went back into the house. I stayed
a few years even after I knew I was on my own.

I Had a Marriage in Those Days

Each row of corn was snug up against
a neighboring row, took its shape
from it, gave its shape to the next row.
When I drove the roads, the corn
ticked by, agreeing on everything.
I'd been told the soil was a kind
called *chernozem*, which takes
centuries to be that dark and fertile,
but I stood in a kitchen on gray
linoleum, layers of wax on it,
layers I myself had added to.
I heard the lambs cry,
penned off for weaning,
a fence keeping them from
the warm udder, the dripping milk.
I didn't know what I was doing those days,
but the marriage began to be clear
in the way a field of corn
will tell the truth
about the lay of the land.
How the corn can't be level
when the land isn't. How it has
its inevitable high places,
its inevitable falling away.

What I Shouted and He Shouted

One or the other has to decide
that's enough, nothing has changed
or it has changed all it can.
The sky is going to be a color

and the moon is going to show up
in some kind of washed-out curve.
The echo of that slap
has made the difference.

We had only walls, rugs, window.
The singing left my body,
that crooked tree
where the singing had wanted to live.

Charmed by the Dirt Road

I was charmed by the dirt road
across a pasture leading to a
farmhouse and his mother
setting two dishpans on the table,
one for washing, the other in which
she stacked everything for rinsing,
pouring water over all from the tea kettle.
I helped. I slipped into my role as
into an apron, drying the plates, cups, forks
with a white dish towel, embroidered:
Sunday, Monday, Tuesday. Perhaps she used
old ragged towels except when I came. When I came
she killed a chicken in the yard and when it was done
flopping, headless, she went to it and took its feet,
carried it, hanging, into the basement,
where she dipped it into a pail of hot water,
tore its feathers off in handfuls,
cut the carcass open on the table she had there,
took the guts out, pulled the lungs loose
from the rib bones, her fingers not lovely
but sure of their task, carried the chicken
upstairs, washed it, the dishpan so useful
again, cut pieces expertly with a thin curved knife,
rolled each drumstick, wing, breast
in flour and laid it into the hot grease of a
cast iron skillet. While it sputtered and browned,

she set the table, stirred up the biscuits
in a green glass bowl. I saw the array:
plates plain and shiny, the cups
waiting for their coffee, all the song of this,
the chorus, the riffs, and I thought
with some minor changes I could do it.

To the Cattle in the Dream

I manage one more time to evade your horns,
those sharp points so close, so often.

Their hook and rip. You in the guise
of friend. Intense eyes and faint praise.

Your gouge and snort, your
suggestion, your help, your well-placed word

into my softness, the pink of my trust.
I've faced you; I've run away.

You paw the ground, but I don't puncture
like I used to. I have fences. There's one now,

and a space beneath the barbed wire
just wide enough for me to roll under.

The Moon Is a Swan

I've heard it called
many things, heard it rhapsodized,
but it has the face of my old teacher
who said I was a time-waster.
How right she was!
Wasted the breath the yellow trees
held one afternoon under their light,
while I did the nit-noise of living,
the errands no one can remember
on the death bed. That's
what the moon is:
a round pale stone death bed
accusing: *What have you done*
with this one more day?
Now comes the cold rain tapping
the shoulders of my coat.
Rain in my eyes when I try
to look up for that swan.

This Is How I Bow Down in Homage

to her, the one who believed in me
while I squandered. I was the wastrel,
trekking down the wrong road,
tossing dollar bills like rose petals
onto the gravel. She hadn't
gone to college but I would,
come hell or high water. Of course
I messed that up, got religious,
took a long time in stained-glass spaces
to learn I didn't belong. I started over.
I was always starting over. But I wouldn't
wear the ecru shirt she sewed,
no matter how careful the seams.
She thought what she had learned
would/should transfer to me.
No. I had to learn the hard way
and she had to watch.

Kindness Scraped Up the Money

Kindness found the money
for what I needed
even after I let her down.
I was a sandbur in her skin. I was

what she dreaded
when she was full of dread in the
lampless night

but when I called one morning,
saying *Come and get me*,
she went to her car;

she drove hours to arrive before
danger came home, banging
through the door. We hurried, she and I.
We left with my small son and a suitcase.

Kindness will do that—
or stubbornness—get up from
her breakfast plate, get on the road,
not taking time to say I told you so.

It's a Small Breath

It's a small breath the bird uses
for its song, intake of air
so light the earth hardly

misses it. Molecules into the beak,
out again, air changed to melody.

I wait for word that he is safe, this heart
of my heart who would not stay home
but sailed, as love is always sailing,

out onto the dark sea.
If he is safe, laughing somewhere

over beer with his friends,
that will be song enough.
And if he is not safe,

no amount of sweet notes
will matter to me.

Not Enough Space in Storage Device

Delete, delete, delete, get rid of everything
I see too often, but then comes a photo:
you wading in the ocean,
   you standing with your palms out,
      doing nothing but looking at me,
        and behind you, waves roll in
      from all the shores the Atlantic touches.
Your shirt drips, clings to your ribs,
   your hair is plastered to your head.
     There, irreplaceable, constant,
       your face wet and welcome.

Hope Springs

There's always the illusion I will
do my to-do list, the never-ending list.
There's the hope for yoga poses
daily, and the power walk. A new
eating plan I'll stick to, the greens
oh the greens. Bread banished
to a hard roll at the end of the week.
Some tall eastern establishment will
worship me with real roses, with bank accounts.
I'll evolve, wear kindness like a long colorful
skirt, even my fingers slimming down,
the grace of dolphins in each wrist.
My teeth will whiten, I'll be strong, I'll not care,
the past dripping off like
swimming-pool water. I'll step
barefoot along the hot tiles,
curl up, big hat, long legs, onto
the chaise lounge of the rest of my life.

From *Learning to Swim*, 2019

Weren't We Beautiful

growing into ourselves
earnest and funny we were
some kind of alien, smiling,
the light we lived in was gorgeous
we looked up and into the camera
the ordinary things we did with our hands
or how we turned and walked
or looked back we lifted the child
spooned food into his mouth
the camera held it, stayed it
there we are in our lives as if
we had all time
as if we would stand in that room
and wear that shirt those glasses
as if that light
without end
would shine on us
and from us.

I Save My Love

I save my love for what is close,
for the dog's eyes, the depths of brown
when I take a wet cloth
to wash his face. I save my love
for the smell of coffee at the Mill,
the roasted near-burn of it, especially
the remnant that stays later
in the fibers of my coat. I save my love
for what stays. The white puff
my breath makes when I stand
at night on my doorstep.
That mist doesn't last, disappeared
like your car turning the corner,
you at the wheel, waving.
Your hand a quick tremble in a
brief illumination. Palm and fingers.
Your face toward me. You had
turned on the overhead light so I would
see you for an instant, see you waving,
see you gone.

Every Last Thing Is Transitory

Today again the cardinal
hopped about on the grass,
red against green. Today again
he flew to the lilac bush
and went into it. Some day
everything will be eaten up
or sunk into a space even darker
than the tar at La Brea. Still,
this morning I vacuumed the floors
which will be gone, I shook rugs,
I unwrapped a new bar of soap.
I am not ready. My daughter,
that creature I love. Not ready
for any goodbye. Her hair,
which I love, supple and dark.
And her hands suddenly still from their
knitting, from counting the stitches
around the circular needle,
her fingers lifting a strand of yarn
and pulling gently to make a little slack
for working. You may have noticed
I am not ready to let go.
The summer we went to the lake.
The day we moved our baggage
from the car to the cabin. I want
that day, all that baggage,
and her feet up the wooden steps,
her arms carrying her baby. I will

not give that. We are slated to disappear like a red bird into green foliage. There has never been anything else, just this everlasting leaving.

Plastic Bag on the Lawn

I was staring into the dark
because I couldn't sleep and then the wind

blew an empty white trash bag
along the ground in the yard. The plastic

moved like a woman
writhing in grief, rolling,

reaching out her arms,
crawling forward,

her head barely rising
then slumping. I stood at the window

and watched what I knew
to be lifeless. I knew what it was

and what it wasn't. It fooled the dog
too. So I knelt beside him

and told him it was okay, listened
to the growling in his throat,

listened to the air
around the shell of the house. Just enough

moonlight to keep the grass dark
and the ghost white. Her legs

caught on the stalk of a rosebush.
She filled and emptied and filled with sorrow.

Edith Porath Nelsen, You Signed Your Quilt

You embroidered your name
in a corner in blue thread after you
sewed these squares together.
You hemmed your quilt, you folded,
you laid it into storage. It came to me,
no blood relation. Edith, I know your name
and your diligence, round and round,
eight stitches to each inch that lies
over my knees. Sometimes, Edith,
I pull your quilt up around my chin and
sit in the yard under constellations.
I listen to silence, I make plans,
as you may have made plans. I save things
I'll never use. I use irreplaceable minutes,
hours. Dark squares from a gray shirt,
squares of rowdy blue flowers. I'll have to
wash this, Edith. It will go into water and suds.
I'm trying to see patterns. Stars I've been told
are belts and swords; I'm trying to see how
it's me, broken stitched to broken.
They tell me to shut up, shut down,
the ever-present *they*, as maybe they told you
and you told others. Edith, I want to keep
going a few more thousand rounds,
to use what I've been given, what came to me,
to squander it in the best way I can,
I want to make it matter.

After the Divorce the Soccer Game

I went to my son's soccer game
he wasn't crazy about soccer but he
always did what he was signed up for
it was a cold day and I had his jacket
but he refused I held that windbreaker
for most of the game it kept its place over my arm
it was a cold day and some of the other kids
were wearing jackets but he wouldn't
he looked cold blue-lipped and his upper arm
was cold when I broke the ancient
iron-clad rule to lay my hand on it
I didn't say a word because at least I knew
some of the rules but I had taken the easy way
the divorce I wanted my son to be warm
waiting to return to battle waiting for the coach
to send him back to run and to fight
and to do the noble thing
which his eyes told me I had not
he shook his head not even the full gesture
just half a head shake only what the game allowed
just half but enough No coat mom never any coat.

What She Taught Me

She taught me linking verbs, predicate nouns,
long division, have a Kleenex ready, an apple
a day. She taught me three-quarter time, Greenwich

Mean Time. She taught me *do re mi*, Mexicali Rose,
Rose, Rose, my Rose of San Antone. She taught me
Peas Peas Peas Peas, Eating Goober Peas.
She taught me that a peanut is a goober pea

in certain parts of the world, that it is fine
for things to be different in different parts
of the world, no two goobers alike in their

dry red skins, their pockmarked pods,
that there are latitudes and longitudes we have
never seen, that she had seen some part,
and so would I, that I need not

forego either hopscotch or baseball, that spelling
is on Friday and it is OK to learn more
than one list, including the hard list; it is not

showing off—it is using what you have.
That using what you have will not please
everybody, that marrying a man of a different stripe

is not a popular thing in a small-town world,
and divorcing and coming home with a child
is even worse, and that you
get up every morning anyway,
and do your work.

To the Author I'm Reading at Night

Because of the way words
sound in the room when I am
sitting up in bed, reading,
I read aloud your tribute to your
teacher, how she saved you,
and knowing that someone somehow
saved *her*,
and someone saved *her*
and so on up the ladder,
not tribute exactly, more than that
and my voice takes a timbre,
a quality from solitude.
I feel I could
understand my mother, how she
loved in a crooked sparkly foolish
deep way and I have that in me too,
my time in the cone of light, my dog
on the end of the bed licking his paw
and knowing nothing, like me,
of hate circling the planet, I'm
forgetting it on purpose and enjoying
this yellow lamplight because someone,
your compassionate teacher, saved you
and you pass it on, black letters in a string,
string after string, to me,

someone alone in a chamber, noise of
traffic outside the walls,
nothing but night in the window,
someone you don't know, reaching
for the rope of that connection.

This Year I Did Not

make the trip to lay flowers
on your grave, no real excuse,
and somehow I hope you won't be

mad. It's as if you're still alive
and I must please you. None of this
is your fault, the pleasing. I can't

make the drive, my reasons
flimsy as curtains billowing
in a spring wind but I loved you

then and now, you of exquisite excuses,
and so I stand in my imagination
in a prairie cemetery where

a bird, unseen, delivers
this morning a complex song, quick notes,
flute-like. Again. No audience but

the plain unadorned grass.
I think you understand.
A bird on the ground

singing, even when refusing
to show herself.

This Is the Photo of My Father Before

he went to war and came home,
before he built a cafe in his small town,
breaking that stunted street open to
hamburgers and French fries and bean soup,
back from military housing and mess halls
to drop down into sepia on paper
and become what he has been ever since:
thin shoulders under a blue shirt,
coffee with cream,
duty with fresh bread, chokecherry jelly,
finish before dark, stay at it
until the last nail is hammered,
stay at it, last log on the pile
sawed and thrown onto the wagon,
last cow milked and headed out the barn door.
But listen, I am tired
of pails of grain and loyalty,
tired of a thousand times when he
washed cups and plates in soapy water
in the kitchen after closing, tired
of each heavy cup following another
and his big fingers handling dishes.
What I loved, I mean,
was that tree, that real thing,
that hackberry he was.
Strength and rough bark,
roots lengthening down into dry loam.

I live my life among the buildings of the city
but when I want, I can think about him,
about mountains, how they
rise from the plains through clouds.
How they endure.

He Taught Me to Drive

The road wasn't a proper road; it was
two ruts across a pasture and down
into a dry creek bed and up

the other side, a cow path really,
soft sand up to the hubcaps.
You didn't gun it at the right time,

he said. I knew that before he
said it, but I didn't know how to get
the old Chevrolet out of the crevice

I had wedged it into. *You'll figure it out,*
he said, and then he took a walk,
left me to my own devices, which until

that moment had been tears.
My face remained nearly dry,
as was the gas tank when he finally

returned, took a shovel out of the trunk,
and moved enough sand from around
the rear tires so he could rock

back and forth and get a little traction.
That country had very little traction;
it had mourning doves, which lay their eggs

on the ground, a few twigs for a nest,
no fluff. Mourning dove. Even the name
sounds soft. Even the notes they coo,

perched on a fence wire. But they are
hatched on the dirt. When they leave the shell,
the wind is already blowing their feathers dry.

I Pretend I Can Remember

It is springtime in Texas when
I am conceived. There is much

sunshine though I can't know sunshine,
cocooned as I am. Sunshine

and puddles of orange flowers
on both sides of all the roads.

Oh how these two love!
The apartment would burst its seams

if they loved one more iota. Unhappy
is what the years will bring

but I don't know that yet,
upside down, growing, getting my nails,

my eyelashes.
Sound of a drum, steady,

and always a noise
like rushing water.

Outside, but very close, he lays his hand or his head
(he is warm and foolish—I will love him)

where she tells him to lay it.

The One with Violets in Her Lap

the one with violets in her lap
—Sappho

is my mother, young, sitting
cross-legged on the grass, my mother
before she tired,
her unbitten hands in her lap, their only job
to hold the flowers or to smooth
her dress over her knees. In a moment
she will be old. A small wind
moves the hem of her skirt.
She sees you coming now across the grass.
Something good happens in her eyes and she
lifts one beautiful cream-colored arm to wave.

For the Record

She was happy and then not happy
and she didn't know how to get happiness back.
Neither of them knew how to get it back.

Skinny legs long arms dark hair blowing
and no smile.
It had been a good smile

as when something unties, unbinds, lets free.
That's what it was like, though there is no record of it.
Let me be the record of it.

The Citrus Thief

Again before daylight
she comes in her robe and pajamas,
her slippers soft on the path,
the circle from her flashlight
bobbing on the ground. She shuts off
the light when she nears the tree.
One orange, cold and hard to her fingers,
will twist off to lie in her palm.
It's the stars, closer than they've
ever been, the ancients
who saw them, the woman who
stepped out of her cave, pulling a pelt
around her shoulders. Cold night,
Milky Way, same for any
future bandit, looking up, starstruck,
with a shred of food in her hand.

Insomnia Is a Streetlight

What is there was there
all along. Something can

light it: a tree flailing in a high wind,
a few leaves swirling down,

the predictable flatness of the sidewalk
where no one is standing but could,

if you choose. *Voila!* There's
somebody in a gray parka, shifting

from one foot to the other in the cold,
someone you used to know or fear or love.

There's the smell of hashbrowns
and bacon in his clothing and hair, this

one you used to walk toward, and with
enough light, can still throw your arms around.

From *The Woman in
the Moon*, 2018

The Nobody Bird

I'm nobody! Who are you?
—Emily Dickinson

The woman leading the bird walk
gets excited because she thinks
for a minute the bird she sees
is one she doesn't have
on her life list
and then she says *Oh it's*
just a dickcissel.
But I raise my binoculars
to bring the sparrow-sized bird,
black throat patch,
dark eye,
into the center of a circle.
I see how the dickcissel
clings to a stem
when he sings, how
he tilts his head back,
opens his throat.
The group follows
the leader to higher ground,
but oh to be
the nobody bird and hang on,
hang on and sing!

My Love With His Saw Has Taken the Cedar Down

I am standing on the stump
where the tree had stood
when he comes around the corner,
sees me motionless, staring,
and asks "Is anything wrong?"
Nothing is wrong.
Everything reaches the end,
aromatic or not,
unmarked or not,
nothing lasts forever,
and it's time for the cedar to go.
It stood all those nights,
all those one o'clocks, two o'clocks,
under the moons I never got up to look at.
The cedar a few thousand nights in the wind
a few feet from where we lay,
he and I, separately dreaming,
or one awake,
listening to the other, breathing.
The cedar he climbed every December
in boots and gloves
when he put up the Christmas lights,
using the limbs, their parallel pattern,
for a ladder to reach the roof.
The cedar was there
hanging on in dry times,
its roots making very small
steady progress

and its molecules lining up densely
purple and deep red and white.
When the tree is opened,
as it is now,
its colors surprising and stark,
out into the air spills
a faint comfort that, like moonlight,
will not quite fade.

When Life Seems a To-Do List

When the squares of the week fill
with *musts* and *shoulds*,

when I swim in the heaviness of it,
the headlines, the fear and hate,

then with luck, something like a slice of moon
will arrive clean as a bone

and beside it on that dark slate
a star will lodge near the cusp

and with luck I will have you
to see it with, the two of us,

fools stepping out the backdoor
in our pajamas.

Is that Venus?—I think so—Let's
call it Venus, cuddling up to the moon

and there are stars farther away
sending out rays that will not

reach us in our lifetimes
but we are choosing, before the chaos

starts up again,
to stand in this particular light.

Each Wrong Choice Was a Horse I Saddled

I rode a little way down the road, got off,
and saddled another,

got better at saddling,
faster at getting on board.

Some of my best days, like today,
all I can do is hang on,

the animal beneath me
galloping in some direction I can't

fathom, my eyes shut,
my rag-doll body flopping,

no stirrups, no reins,
my fingers in the mane,

my most recent egregious error
trying so hard to buck me off.

What I Think My Real Self Likes

She likes to stand in left field
on a day with no ball game,
only crows on thousands of blades of grass.

She likes—I think she likes—
a park at midnight,
clouds trailing over the cheeks of the moon,

showing the light, hiding it.
That kind of flirting she likes.
She grabs my to-do list

from the counter and beats me with it.
Stop making this crappy fuss,
she says, and stomps off

in her red leather boots.
I hate the sound of it, you know
what I mean: the quiet
after she slams the door.

My Mother the Child

She didn't get her hand stuck
and chopped off in the corn picker;
she didn't make headlines that way
but there must have been
a day something happened
to the unmarked child she was,
something I can't reach back
and save her from,
and it, or he,
got her,
wrung her turtledove heart
or filled her mouth and eyes
with fear, which drained away
of course but which also
settled, like water
in the aquifer, to influence
what would flourish above the surface
in the rows:
cabbages big as washtubs,
radishes waiting to be pulled up by the tops,
onions sweet as apples, and yet something
sometimes shriveled the pears on the tree.
An oriole moved among the empty branches.

What He Needed

I told my father about a study
that showed pain was relieved
by laughter to be more specific by
belly laughs it was a stupid
thing but I was desperate and
that's what the article said
he was in so much pain I wanted
to help him if I could I told him
some people reported a few
hours of good sleep after
laughing really hard there was a ratio
number of minutes laughing
to number of minutes they could sleep
he could have said any number of things he
could have said you have no inkling
no fraction of an idea about pain
so bad you wish you were dead
he had in fact stopped eating
he had in fact decided to escape
the tubes in his arm his tag-along
monitor ticking like a Martian
and to go home to his green recliner
his north window his old dog
to be more specific he said will you
help me he said will you get my shoes
he said that right before I betrayed him
to a nurse to tell the truth I was afraid
an impossible coward I wasn't in the habit

of lying to him but I made as if I were going to
get his shoes those brown dress shoes he had worn
to the hospital those which he had pushed his feet
into and leaned over in old man pain and tied
I couldn't I was the turncoat
the enemy had brainwashed and I turned him in
told the young nurse intent on her computer
she rose up and went to his room and I
came at her heels traitor-like his one last
chance to walk out on two legs
when in fact he needed a buddy he
needed a daughter he needed his shoes.

Final Shirt

After my father died, my mother
and my sisters picked the shirt, the tie;
he had just the one suit.
I left them to it, I didn't
want to choose, I loved him
all those years. They took a shirt
from the closet, I don't remember
which one, I'm sure he had worn it
to church and hung it up again.
They held a tie against the cloth
of the shirt. They decided, finally.
It's like that. Things come down
to the pale blue or the white,
or some other. Someone buttoned it
over him, those buttons he had unbuttoned.

Despair Woke Me

Despair woke me in the night,
the yard quiet, moon not yet risen,
trees and sky waiting. I looked for
the stars I knew, not many, naming some
to comfort myself: little
Rigel, red Antares, fuzzy Polaris,
though each could already be a cinder or
burning at such a distance as never to warm me,
and I happened to think of him
as if to bring up from the horizon
what he said one day in particular,
at the door to a very plain room
long ago disassembled,
existing nowhere anymore.
A small set of words, each following each,
to make me smile in the dark.

Ah, Charles, If You Could Have

C.C. 1967–1987

If you could be in the known world
this morning, peeling this orange,

the cover of it giving way in pieces.
The aroma, Charles, the tang,

even the color of the thin rind. I wish
you had felt it was worth it,

my good, my handsome, my clean-cut boy.
I know I can't know

how unbearable the days became,
the nights, tearing along lines unseen.

The sweet, the sharp, can't they
on occasion reach across a gap?

Won't some small common thing
sometimes keep us here?

What Did You Think Love Would Be?

When you pushed him out into air
or rather your body did it all
by itself, as it had formed him
a seed in its pod, complete,
sleeping mostly, sometimes
the perfect jeweler's hammer
of his foot against the womb
and you could feel that language,
the soft notes which
his heels had for words. And
today he has his own work to do,
the hours, the papers and screens
to fill with symbols,
once in a while a message
you to him, him to you:
weather, schedules, taps
against the wall. Perhaps
love is a canvas, syllables
brush strokes, spots of color
in the whole, and you can
pick them out, can see them,
their particular hue among the many:
here and *here* and *here.*

About That Smart Thinly Veiled Stuff

That smart thinly veiled stuff
I said to my daughter—
my admiration was real as eggs in the nest
but my goal was to save her.
I wonder if my mother, too, had that intent.
Let me, in the time I have left,
love my daughter
and keep my hands off.
Let me say a simple thing
and mean a simple thing.
Let a word be a round pebble
passed from one hand to another,
a little weight in the palm,
not a burden, not a door,
not a justification,
not advice covered up
with a blue scarf.
Let me love her as a bird might
value the tree and the rain.

My Daughter Tells Me She Loves Me

It's after I make a big mistake
(again) trying to be helpful.
It's that she will have to negotiate traffic
the squirrely intersections
to deliver what I forgot.
It's late, it's hot, the back lot
of a motel, where I'm waiting
in my robe and pajamas
for her, for the hand-off. I'm
waiting near the overflowing dumpsters
a game of dodgeball going on
in dim light, parked cars
shouts of children.
It's what I can't fix
and can only tangle further
it's what can fix it
she gets out of her car,
leaves the door hanging open
there isn't time there isn't
time but she says it,
the only thing there is time for
in the bone-tired heat and sweat of July
I love you, Mom
the tangle the knot
it really is all right.

Green Ash

I took a place, rooted
where I found myself
and rose, steady with rain and sun
and rain again. There were machines
but I did not look toward them,
faced sky with its cloud shapes,
drew up water until it flowed
in every vein and twig, I made
green of it, let birds build, come and
go, as if they were my only voice.
I gestured, waved, moved
with midnight storms, felt tall,
kept going, knuckle of new branches.
I held snow, dropped it,
reached up and out. This is gone now.
In concentric rings I remember.

My Notes in Margins

My notes in margins,
along the edges of the text,
the ink I've left. Who

did I do that for?
Myself. Only myself. As if to say
you will live long enough

to read this page again
and you'll see what you
marveled at then

and compare it to
how you feel now.
The dust of the comet's

tail coming around in
orbit again. An intersection.
What was

meets what is, and,
for a second,
shines.

From *I Have Nothing to Say about Fire*, 2016

The Track the Whales Make

You and I on the boat notice
the track the whales leave,
the huge ring their diving draws
for a time on the surface.
I want to believe
when we can no longer
walk across a room
for a hug, can no longer
step into the arms of the other,
there will be this:
some delicate trace that stays.
And below, out of sight,
dark mammoth shadow
flick of flipper
body of delight
diving deep.

She Gives Me the Watch Off Her Arm

my mother wants me
to go to college

the closest she has ever been
is this—
the dorm

her father had needed her
to dig the potatoes
and load them into burlap bags

but here she is
leaving her daughter

on the campus in the city time to go
we are at the desk
the clerk is wide-

eyed when my mother
asks her if she will
take an out-of-town check

if the need arises
if something comes up
so my girl will have money

even I know
this isn't going to happen

this check-cashing

a clerk helping me with money
but miracle of miracles
the clerk says nothing

and I say nothing
and my mother feels better
we go to the parking lot

old glasses thick graying hair
she is wearing a man's shirt
has to get back to the job

we stand beside her Ford and it is
here she undoes the buckle of the watch
and holds it out to me

my father's watch
keeping good time for him
and then for her

she says she knows I will
need a watch to get to class
we hug and she gets in

starts the car
eases into traffic
no wave

the metal of the back of the watch

is smooth to my thumb
and it keeps for a moment
a warmth from her skin

The Story, Part of It

The story, part of it, is that
the tractor was parked, running,
at the top of the hill, and
my sister Jennie, ten years old, climbed
up and took a seat at the wheel. The story,
part of it, is that my father worked on something
attached behind the tractor, the digger or the chain
perhaps; the story does not tell all. It tells
what he said to Jennie, his instruction; it tells
what he said into the fierce wind blowing that day,
the roar of the wind and the roar of the tractor.
He said Whatever you do, don't step on the clutch.
The wind took his words, flipped and turned them,
gusted them even as it gusted everything,
even as it tossed the ends of the red scarf Jennie wore,
flapping it out and back, out and back. Jennie
heard him say Step on the clutch, and she did.
The tractor lurched down the hill like an animal
freed. The story, part of it, tells how the tractor
rolled, gaining, how Jennie stood steadfast
on the clutch, hanging onto the wheel, her hair
and her red scarf flying with the speed of it, how
the tractor sped down the slope until it
hit the barbed wire fence at the bottom,
broke through and rolled over,
how she flew off, and the clutch engaged and
killed the engine. Everything was at that second
silent from the roaring, and Jennie was

face down on the grass, alive, but he, my father,
thought she was dead.
And years later when my father was dying, I called
Jennie. You'd better come, I said. She arrived
at the hospital and I met her at the main door
to show her through the maze, the halls,
to my father's last room. We turned the turn
and could see him ahead. No longer
a man at work. Or rather a man doing
the new work of dying. He sat in the bed, tubes
into the skin of the backs of his hands.
He looked up and caught
sight of her, of us, and then he did what
Jennie cannot explain, get over, understand,
make sense of: he put his hand over his eyes;
he looked down at the floor while we came to him.
The story, part of it, is that Jennie cannot let go of this.
She told me: It's what he's always done—
he did not want to see me, to look at me.
No, I told her. No, it was to keep from crying.

How I Left You

I walked to the river and stood
on the bridge at sundown

long strings of cranes
wavered toward me

long knotted strings
and the trilling of thousands

I went as a cheetah I left
home I went as a hawk I could see you

below I went as a seed from this
world each time I went out I

swallowed you you swallowed me
sleek in my gorgeous spots

I went as the milky way I overflow
I hide in my glorious coat.

Bad News, Good News

I was at a camp in the country,
you were home in the city,
and bad news had come to you.

You texted me as I sat
with others around a campfire.
It had been a test you and I

hadn't taken seriously,
hadn't worried about.
You texted the bad news word

cancer. I read it in that circle
around the fire. There was
singing and laughter to my right and left

and there was that word on the screen.
I tried to text back but,
as often happened in that county,

my reply would not send, so I went to higher ground.
I stood on a hill above the river and sent you
the most beautiful words I could manage,

put them together, each following each. Under
Ursa Major, Polaris, Cassiopeia, a space station flashing,
I said what had been said

many times, important times, foolish times:
those words soft-bodied humans say when the news is bad
the *I love you* we wrap around our

need and hurl at the cosmos: Take this, you heartless
nothing and everything, take this.
I chose words to fling into the dark toward you

while the gray-robed coyote came out of hiding
and the badger wandered the unlit hill
and the lark rested herself in tall grasses;

I sent the most necessary syllables
we have, after all this time the ones we want to hear:
I said *Home*, I said *Love*, I said *Tomorrow*.

Thanksgiving for Two

The adults we call our children will not be arriving
with their children in tow for Thanksgiving.
We must make our feast ourselves,

slice our half-ham, indulge, fill our plates,
potatoes and green beans
carried to our table near the window.

We *are* the feast, plenty of years,
arguments. I'm thinking the whole bundle of it
rolls out like a white tablecloth. We wanted

to be good company for one another.
Little did we know on our first picnic
how this would go. Your hair was thick,

mine long and easy; we climbed a bluff
to look over a storybook plain. We chose
our spot as high as we could, to see

the river and the checkerboard fields.
What we didn't see
was this day, in our pajamas if we want to,

wrinkled hands, wine
in juice glasses, toasting
whatever's next,

our decades side-by-side,
our great good luck.

We Disagree

Your chin took on that particular jut
I would come to know,

white stone above the innocent plaid
of your collar. You were

mashing the potatoes, we had your parents
coming for dinner, I was making gravy, had

taken off my blouse to prevent spots. I,
in a black bra and red apron, you in

strength and righteousness. We were
interesting, arguing. You

manhandled the pot of potatoes,
threw in a slab of butter, poured in milk.

You beat the bejesus out of those spuds,
the beater clacking

with every stroke. *Beat beat beat,*
your biceps fine, rounded, a vein

visible under the skin, your face
stern above the potatoes. I whisked the

roux in the cast iron skillet, turned up
the heat. It was impasse

but I knew they'd be here any minute
and we had to be a happy couple

so I poured in lots of broth
and stirred like my grandmother

to make everything smooth
in time to put my shirt back on.

Let Me Think of the Frost That Will Crack Our Bones

Let me think of how I ruined
Christmas Eve one year when I would not

let slide what you said,
again. I was wearing

the blue robe you gave, wearing it
over my sweater and jeans, my feet

in the new slippers for the first
of thousands of times. I wish I had walked

into the yard to look at the stars, Pleiades perhaps,
that cold cluster of lights far from the warm

fragrant stubborn righteous vindicated
folds and limbs and symmetry of our selves.

Perhaps you would have followed me or
I would have called you to look at what is

so very distant and in that manner—that
or some other ploy—I could have

maneuvered you close to me,
the heat and welcome of your body.

Draw What Is There

In art class, the instructor says
Draw your hand—not an idea of hand

but what is really there.
My pencil scratches over paper,

telling the truth. Wrinkles.
Crookedness and bulges.

I let the ring fall to the side,
as it often does, let the tunneling

veins go where they have to go,
but left out is this:

the day I pulled your hair,
my son,

when you broke something.
It was too much, all of it.

Not the green plastic
forgettable trifle you broke;

I mean my work, my union with your father.
It was too much and it was too little

and you were there, young and perfect
and close by my hand. You say

you don't remember
so I don't mention it again

but I remember and
have not let it go.

Let me turn my hand over, watch
the ends of the fingers catch light,

notice that knuckles are only creases
over the bones that do the work.

Let me see what is
in front of me, opening and closing.

Let what I did and failed to do
drop like a leaf from my hand.

Those Pieces We Carry

My mother carried a leather purse, stashed it
under her arm, brought it out when needed

like the dry cough she used
in a roomful of strangers, a church, any

uncomfortable place. She had a dog, Moose,
one of several Chihuahuas in the dynasty.

Moose's toenails ticked down the hall,
his ears up as if to help him fly,

hind half wagging, eyes shining.
My mother was eager

but afraid, sure she'd be stepped on.
She needed protection and warmth,

sitting up in the hospital bed,
her hands empty. *I had a little dog where is it*

she asked me. I had the advantage of health
and organized answers.

I sat in a chair beside her bed
and explained everything.

What I Think My Father Loved

He signed up,
walked in a line to the troop carrier.

Newly shorn. New scratchy uniform.
I think he loved the green of the island

and he loved the ocean. He told me he watched
a native float like a log in the surf. My father

on the shore, working, looking up
from time to time to see him floating,

rising on a wave, white foam
lapping over, dissolving, reforming.

When the man came out of the water,
my father spoke to him, asking

how to float and ride like that.
The answer: *Don't tell the ocean what to do.*

When my father's work was done,
the beach was dark. I imagine him

wading in, a barely visible line of foam
coming toward him like a greeting.

I imagine him, farm boy from a different
hemisphere, his feet leaving the bottom,

his body lying back in the bed of the water,
ocean lifting and turning,

ocean holding him loosely,
rolling him.

It Does Not Have to Be Worth the Dying

I'd been at the cabin, resting
on an inner tube in the lake or
lying on a towel in the shade,
listening to the motor boats and
the slow stirring of leaves
in the cottonwoods. I'd been sleeping
all night with the windows open,
been walking barefoot on hot sand,
standing in the kitchen in my swimsuit, fixing
sandwiches for kids. Sunday,
on the ride home, I watched cornfields
roll by. Suddenly against the slope of a field:
a vision. I saw my father's head, large, his eyes
closed, and I knew what it would be
for me when he died, when that love went
out, that form gone, closed, done.
I wrote, tears running, cheeks wet,
wrote and wrote as if to stop it
or keep it. Later my friend said
one should never write about that,
your father dying; you invite these
things to happen. But I knew she was
wrong. The leaves turn and churn
slowly all night in the cottonwoods.

The lake is deep under
the sky whether or not we wake
and hear waves slapping the sand,
whether or not we rouse up and see
a patch of light the moon makes,
a shimmer floating on the water.

Last Day of Kindergarten

In the photograph
the boy is ecstatic,
set free, a young king,
everything ahead of him.
There is nothing he can't have
if he wants it, and he wants it,
as does his friend beside him.
They are ready now to ride off
together and slay dragons,
rescue the world. It's all here
in the park after the last bell;
it's here in the green summer
they have been released to.
It's here in their manhood.
They've only finished kindergarten
but they understand freedom
and friendship. They're on top
of the picnic table, they're on top
of the world in their tennis shoes,
they have raised their arms,
they are such men as could
raise continents; they have
survived. Look how their
fingers reach the sky
and their legs are sure as
horses. Their bodies
will forever do anything they ask.

For My Daughter

When they laid you on my belly

and cut the cord

and wrapped you and gave you

to my arms, I looked into the face

I already loved. The cheekbones,

the nose, the deep place

the eyes opened to. I thought

then this is the one I must teach,

must shape and nurture.

I was sure I should. How was I

to know you would become

the one to show me

how kindness walks in the world?

Some days the daughter

is the mother,

is the hand that reaches

out over the pond, sprinkling

nourishment on the water.

Some days I am the lucky koi,

rising from below, opening

the circle of my mouth to take it in.

From *Losing the Ring in
the River*, 2013

Clara Says I Do

I take a loaf from the oven, cut it, and
the hot slice topples slowly into my hand.

I store salt in a dish in the cupboard
so I can reach in and get a pinch

to sprinkle over eggs in a skillet.
I wash diapers. I wash chore clothes

smelling of pig barn. Every Monday I
clean the clothesline, running a rag over it;

the hand with the rag I raise above my head,
my feet treading the ground.

And that is how I think of myself:
one fist skyward, walking.

I shake the wrinkles out of a wet shirt and hang it.
When it fills like a sail, I run my hand

for a second over its cotton back
before I go on.

Clara Loses the Ring

Frying eggs in bacon fat this morning,
I think about it.
I don't like to think about it,

the river filling my mouth and throat,
my hands clawing the water,
clawing his arm; he is mad

about that, the scratches on his arm,
and he is mad about the ring,
said he will never buy me another,

said I have a ring if I can find it
at the bottom of the river.
In part of my mind

I think it was not my fault,
he shouldn't have been holding
my head under and laughing

but he does that kind of thing. It was
supposed to be fun, cooling off
in the river after a hot day in the field.

Nothing can make him sorry,
not the least bit. I baste the eggs,
blindfolding them the way he likes,

splashing bacon grease over them
with my mother's old spatula. Brown flecks
catch and hold on the yolks. Maybe with time

he'll come to be more loving and kind.

When I Have Hurt Him as Much as I Can

When I have fingered the slingshot
lodged for so long in my pocket;

when I have picked up a stone he,
beleaguered, has dropped in passing;

when I have aimed at the white patch of skin
between his pale blue eyes;

when I have pulled back and let loose;
when my stone, sharp-cornered as a word,

sinks in and in,
when its burn equals

some of the wounds I carry,
then as our mothers and fathers did

he will lie down lonely
and I will lie down lonely,

touching through the blanket.
Distance enough, distance enough.

Potato Soup

turn the peelings in long ribbons
into the metal pan
not quite under your breath curse him

say he is pigheaded and tight
say he should not expect it say
nowhere in the gold locket
opening to the strong dark face
did it promise you would
run down bugs in a house not
fit for the goat woman

nowhere in the new grass the crickets
the stars did it prophesy coal dust

say your mother warned you
against Irish against strong fingers

chop them into convenient sizes
the potatoes the onions
she warned he would smell of onions

while it is boiling throw
the peelings to the chickens
wipe your hand on your coat
not even a decent henhouse

milk and butter and salt
float the pepper on the top
turn the gas low at least it's
not cobs

slice an apple for the canary
it hasn't sung for days

rock

the squeak of the wood comforts as
the light goes down
and down

on the east wall the everyday
pattern of lace and cedar branches
fading

rise

stir

the children are gone except Davy
Charles is dead under this snow

when he opens the door tell him
it is ready.

I Was New and Shiny

When I was new and shiny
and the river was a sister
who liked my least idea,

when winter's sweet cold air
called me out at night
to test the ice along the edges,

I built a fire on the bank
and sat before it,
my old blue coat almost warm enough.

November's fire, November's ground.
I roasted an apple on a fork;
the fruit darkened in the flames,

gave its perfume.
Juice sputtered and fizzed
out the holes in the skin.

The stars held their close cold mirth
or rather

their tinsel promise.
Some folks will tell you they hear voices, even melodies.
Oh why aren't I what I wanted to be?

Playing My Cards

The head of the snake sways,
its body coils

in the garden,
its rattles shake out a noise.

I raise my hoe high,
the tongue of the snake

flickers, and I strike.
Down comes my blade

like a judgment.
The headless body

whips in the row of onions,
whips slower, slower. I contemplate

the cards I've been dealt;
the conversation flows on. I see a way

if I can manage, just three,
just two,

just this one more trick past the
unsuspecting Luke who

is so intent on winning.
Ah, the jack! That does it. No

stopping me now. Swiftly the
ace, king, queen, and ten.

To all holding cards around this table:
what, exactly, sits here among you,

who, exactly, I will become,
none of us has any idea.

Let Me Be the First Snake of Spring

Let me writhe, immodest

Let me be a long white underbelly

Against the warm wrist of the garden

Circle what can be circled

Be hard, be narrow, be cold

Let me not care

Let the proper wish me away

Let me find their houses

Their stairways in the sun

Their furrows, their lettuces

Let me flick my tongue into the air of

The world which does not love me

Which praises emptiness

Which would step and stomp

With heavy brown boots

Which with any tool at hand

Would be glad

To break the quick coils

Of my beautiful spine.

To the Moon in the Morning

Moon in the morning, chunk of ice melting,
moon wearing no sandals
and half your dress gone, too:

Come, breakfast with me.
Dance this mimosa down your throat
in my garden of hollyhocks.

No. Don't come. Don't bother. You're like
any other Puritan piece of rock, turning your back
when I show up in a towel

to lie in my hammock. O icy moon of Decency,
never lived on the plains in the summertime,
find your own long-stemmed champagne.

I'll outlast you, Honey,
outlast August and a stinky neighborhood.
Think I'll pay through the nose for my nakedness?

See if I care. Ah but Liebchen,
come closer, warm up. Melt,
you little ice chip, between my heavy breasts.

Note to My Father After All These Years

Today I spend money. Doodad this, doodad that
in a town in the sun on the border. I sit

outdoors with my doodad dog
at the coffee shop. Time passes.

A man casts a shadow across my latte,
asks if he can borrow my lighter for a minute.

I have none but he talks to me anyway,
generous with conversation,

his tattooed hands giving my dog some
good attention. I can't see his eyes,

only the dark of his sunglasses. His unlit cigarette
bobs in his lips as he talks. This,

or something, reminds me of you. He says
the people here are nice. He loves it here,

says it's way better than the big city; it's all
money anyways; every time he left the house

it was forty bucks. He sees someone
across the street, waves his arm,

shouts: *Jack, I'm free!*
He rises. He's gone.

I Leaned in Close

My mother lay in her hospital bed;
I leaned in close and burrowed my hands
under her back. It was the best hug
we could manage and we managed it.
She was worried about where I would sleep—
that old groove again—and how far
the motel was. Instead of saying something
important and eternal, I said it was nearby.
I said I had my car and she double-checked
all that. She thought I was in danger,
so instead of going
I stayed and we filled a vial of time,
a small glass tube, the way you can carry around
a dram of the Indian Ocean in your purse.
I reaffirmed which light she wanted on
and repositioned the nurse call button.
I told her the motel was just down the road
and leaned over her again,
took her bones in my arms
and kissed her face.

Take, Eat; This Is My Body

Take, eat; this is my body,
now when you are forming
cell by cell,

small crusts,
the fine chain of your spine.
Lashes, eyelid, brow.

Fingers curling, anthers
of tropical flowers.
Take, eat.

This is a way I love you,
unseen earwig, growing. I will be
blue-white milk at your mouth.

I will be a shadow on a building,
the low sun casting a shape
behind me as I go on.

You and I, the Cranes, the River

The cranes were silhouettes that night, thousands
lowering in long strings to land in the shallow river.
We stood at peepholes in a shed on the bank,

silent, watching. And I began to wish
someone could see us, witness us, you and I,
durable in our heavy coats and scarves,

looking out into darkness. We were not jaded then.
Nothing remarkable happened for an hour,
no talking; we didn't want to spook the cranes

standing on their sandbars, trilling their
all-night song. Then you pointed
toward a peephole in the western wall,

turned my shoulders, mouthed a word,
one word. Vapor rose from your mouth. *Moon*, you said.
We looked at it together, a thin white curved tusk,

a filament, a lost string, a moon on its back.
At a small window we looked at the moon together.

From *Beside You at the Stoplight*, 2010

Pulling Up Beside My Husband
at the Stoplight

We are going to the same place
but we take two cars.
Sunday morning and there's not much traffic
so I pull up beside him at the stoplight. There he is
in his car, beside my car,
his profile in the window,
the brown of his hair against his neck. He turns
and blows me a kiss. I watch it float on by.
I motion for another.
I'm remembering how he comes into the dark bedroom
each weekday morning,
the sound of his workboots across the carpet,
the scent of his face when he finds me in the covers,
kisses my eyebrow and the corner of my mouth,
tells me the weather report
and the precise time of day.
So I roll down my window, whistle in my throat,
pull my glasses crooked on my face,
do my best baboon snorting,
pound the horn as if it were bread dough.
There is only the woman in the white Buick
but he is embarrassed, glad to see the green.
I'm stepping on the gas, catching up,
wondering what I can do at 56th and Calvert.

Weekends, Sleeping In

No jump-starting the day.
No bare feet slapping the floor
to bath and breakfast.

Dozing instead in the nest,
like, I suppose,
a pair of gophers

underground
in fuzz and wood shavings.

One jostles the other in closed-eye luxury.
We are, perhaps, at last
what we are:

uncombed, unclothed, mortal.
Pulse and breath and dream.

Even the Alphabet

Consider *s*
who stands beside another, close as possible,
c who will not abandon *k* at the end,
no matter how thick the attack,
q who breaks the trail for *u*, who without *u*
can hardly manage what is required—
and consider how letters live in the body,
play in it, against the back of the teeth,
in the wet active tongue,
and make the lips to part, to close.
Consider how necessary silence is,
coupled with constancy,
how silence can make a word benign
so that it does not shout to show valor,
but softly stands in place
and changes everything,
as does *k* who, though it can speak,
kneels before *n* and says nothing, nothing.

On the Road

My father knew of a store on the highway
where they sold good bologna
so we stopped there—what is better
than a working man on vacation?

It was better than it should be, all of it:
the gray road,
pale hot land rolling by the windows,
two buckskin horses at a fence,

the shine of my young mother's hand
as she cut the bologna with a jackknife,
the tips of her fingers placing a circle of meat
on the cracker, placing a crumble of cheese,

a woman laughing,
a man in love, driving,
his mouth open to receive
the wafer from her hand.

Template

I saw my father sag on the stairs,
break like a couple of sticks,
and weep, a few tears

down his face near his nose,
his eyes shut,
his arms at his sides,

and my mother stood
a few feet away
making pie crust in a bowl,

her fingers
pinching flour and Crisco
and the dash of salt.

Her chin
the chin of her one-legged grandfather,
his crutch down and forward

and down again,
crossing the yard to the barn
where he couldn't pitch hay

but could manage,
with cursing and grit,
to milk a Holstein.

My mother can mutter
with her lips practically closed.
My father can cry on the stairs

and none of my words
can lift him
or make my mother's hands

stop shaping and rolling
and turning the flat white circle of pie crust,
dragging it limp through flour.

I Didn't Know I Loved

I didn't know I loved her big hands
slicing iceberg lettuce
with a thick-bladed knife,

loved her thumb hooked over the lip
of the shallow Melmac bowl
she carried to the table.

Low-class no-class entrees
like her Swiss steak,
her bean soup in a kettle.

She posed in shorts and a halter top,
goosebumps on her white legs.

My father loved her,
carried the photograph away to war,
brought it back.

I didn't know I loved open country,
prairie grass,
miles and miles of sky.

The coyote's unstudied lope across the field.
The badger's un-pretty teeth,
its front door a hole in the gully.

My mother made cottage cheese.
Why did I never tell you this before?

She left the bowl of milk overnight
on the counter, added rennet.
I sprinkled sugar on the clots and ate it.

I didn't know I loved the head of the nail,
the blow of the hammer,
blueprints become the shell of the house.

The foot into the same shoe each morning
six days a week,
leather taking the contour of arch.

I didn't know I loved
the way a red-tailed hawk
will sit in a tree, waiting

to swoop down and to crush
any live warm thing that will nourish.

Stand-In

My mother, on her back, struck at the nurses
during the ambulance ride. *Combative*
was the word they checked on their form.
She tried to black their eyes.
She didn't use her famous silent treatment,
so successful so many times;
she used her fists, those old crumpled leaves,
and she aimed for what was above her.
She slapped the best schools,
the up market, the down market,
the classmate
who wore the red sash on the white dress.
She scratched at the woman who could waltz,
the one who had the pretty laugh.
Just this once the handsome face of money
hung almost within reach
of her work-red short-nail bad-luck hands.
Combative, the nurse tells me, and I say I'm sorry,
but a part of me I usually ignore
speaks up;
a part of me I often discount
says, *No, you're not.*

She Was Perhaps Dead

She was perhaps dead
and the pacemaker kept her heart pumping.
Her eyes stared like nothing I'd seen
and her jaw clamped; she was biting her lip.
The nurses, knowing where to press,
made her let go somehow.
She never blinked. She stared
like an actress in a silent movie.
The hospice staff knew
how to turn the pacemaker off,
my sisters holding a magnet
over the device under the skin
of her thin chest.
I stood away and cried.
There is much I can do
but I couldn't do that,
though I touched her skin
before and after it was cold,
laid my warm palms
on her hands.
You worked hard, Mom, I said,
and I said, *Thank you*.
I held my sisters while they cried.
One, then the other
in my arms—
I held those who had held her.

Labor

My mother picked up a piece of clotted blood,
wiped it from the floor with a Kleenex,
a motion of stooping down and scooping up.
She followed me down the hall
of the small-town hospital

and she probably knew the names of the people
in the chairs in the waiting area, but I didn't.
I knew only the pains of labor
and that I had been waiting hours and hours
for all this to be over,

no husband to hold my hand,
and I walked the hall
because the nurse thought walking might help.
I held my back and held my front,
that hobbling holding groaning posture of motherhood

and motherhood also following it,
mopping up its spill,
its red stain
while the doctor
goes home for Sunday dinner. Motherhood is

pain in regular increments:
something to be stayed with,
to be trailed in its wobbly circles,
its keening cry followed,

until it can lie carefully and heavily down and deliver.

Textile

Where are those scraps
which warmed us?
Women's work

quilts are, and do not last.
Steel persists,
and silver.

Cotton goes the way of rivers,
snowbanks,
footprints,

sweethearts, all of it
mere embroidery.
Cotton is mortal,

takes meaning
from the threads
around it,

travels over and under,
breaks open,

burns,
exhales,

gives its ash to air.

For My Body

Belly, thank you, holding whatever grief I feed on.
What to do with the corn chips, the almonds, the late-night bread?

Arms: hanging on until you crumble.
Neck: stiff, afraid of plunder.

Spine and ribs, all my bones,
lusty, involved.

All pouches, blossoms, chutes, sinews, cul-de-sacs, seedpods
waiting for harvest, thank you.

The son you bore
drove up and parked in front of the house at Christmas.

How giddy, how foolish the body
leaving the kitchen, the food roasting or boiling or waiting,

metatarsals shoeless
down the sidewalk to greet him,

iris and pupil and retina
working as if to remember this:

his body in his gray parka, getting out of the car,
keys in his hand,

his arms reaching to hold
as your arms reach to hold.

Body: storehouse of the infinite,
giddy, foolish, forgiven.

I Want to Be a Man

I want my voice deep out of my chest
water welling up in a spring. Hard water. Rock
dissolved in it. A good-looking man, why not?
I want excellent teeth. Tough skin.
I want a beard. I want shirts. I want biceps.
I want to play basketball as if it mattered,
pound down the court, life or death.
My hair in a ponytail,
or maybe no hair at all.
I want to take my guitar out of the case,
thread my arm and neck through the strap,
sing a baby-baby song. I want to cook,
want to chop onions with a big knife, chop fast,
as the onion and the knife and the board
seem to need. I want to cook four-alarm chili, I want to
eat it. I want to eat jalapeno. I want to sweat.
On my legs I want hair—I mean *hair*, I mean
bristles. Whatever I carry—
the plates, the ladder, the log—
will be light as peanuts.

I don't want to be a man.
Oh, I want the shirt and the sweat and the chilis,
the chest hair and baby-baby. I want that, as I want all.
I want to weep, man and woman, and to be done weeping,
filled and empty at the same time.

Man and woman and animal and vegetable and mineral,
I want to write my songs. I want to break open,
a papaya full of black seeds. I want to pour out
red as wine into raised cups.

You Can't Say *I*

Resist much.
—Walt Whitman

Imagine the authorities telling us we can't say *I*.
Imagine the fines I'll have to pay:
500 for *I will*, 500 for *I want*, 500 for *Do I*?

And then the next decree
comes down: no *my*, no *mine*.
You, *my* friend, friend of *mine*,
may have a stash of *I* and *me*
jingling around like quarters

but authority can clip a hole in the pocket of your jeans
with sharp silver scissors. You still have a *Could I* and a *Should I*
hidden in one pair of shoes, under the arch supports.
Walk around on that.

There have always been people telling us you can't say *I*.
What do they say, I wonder, to their mirrors in the morning
or when they sit in their meetings?

There have always been people like us, common as grass,
who stand with the best posture they can muster
and sometimes hold hands or link arms
and walk down the road hearing a beat in the body,
one foot saying *I*, the other saying *we*.

Mammogram

My name is Maggie, she says, *and I'll be*
doing your mammogram today.
Maggie all day in a windowless room
saying dozens of times: *I'm just*
going to have you step up here—now if you'll
turn a little to your right, put your arm here.

She lifts my left breast, the one with the vague densities
my doctor wants a closer look at. She lays it
on a cold steel shelf.
Her foot presses a switch; a piece of Plexiglas,
a colorless flat hand,

whines down, thins my breast,
flattens it under plastic into a fat living capital A,
the nipple stretched like a maroon stocking cap
at the top of big A.
Maggie's foot taps, the A spreads,
big A, bigger A, humongous A.
How's that? she asks.
Don't breathe, she says

and steps behind her shield, pushes buttons.
You can breathe now, she says,
but I have been, a little, all along, for luck.
She is going to show these to the radiologist
and would I wait right here?
In my tissue-paper gown, I wait.

I half take off the gown and do my own exam:
you look good to me; you look fat and sleek
and happy as a baby,
you with three black dots
where Maggie marked with her felt tip.
Hey you, I say, *you're good. You're both* OK.

Sure enough Maggie comes back and she says
Everything's fine. And though
I think she means the X-rays are readable, not fuzzy,
I'll take it.
Yes, Maggie, I'm fine. Both right and left,
I'm fine past the lady at Information,

I'm fine out the revolving door.
Fine on South 27th,
and fine at Commercial Federal where the cashier
asks me how I am today.

And re-inflated, having found in a pocket early this morning
an old check I forgot to cash,
and having cashed it,
and having the day off,
and having left and right in all their densities
against my favorite washed-out purple shirt,

and having no stainless steel Plexiglas callbacks
for at least six months,
I tell the cashier: I'm fine.
I'm truly fine.

You Wonder Why We Don't Get Along

I'm bromegrass, bluestem,
lespedeza like a fur ball in the hand.
Nine-Mile Prairie is my hangout. I live there,
weekends, with the ticks and the jaybirds,
with the swallow's slow arc
from cedar to cedar.

I'm the Platte, crossing and
re-crossing its own channels.
I'm a prairie liar; I learned to walk
on switchgrass, on cactus,
toddling after my grandfather
checking on his cattle.
Barefoot—silly baby—I couldn't keep up,

and then his Herefords turned and charged.
I'm used to the blank stare.
A snort in the nostrils is
my lullaby. I'm running still,

unshod feet
over unplowed ground.
No screams from my mouth: open,
soft as the evening primrose.
Silent, chased by my herd.

Her Kid Brother Ran Beside the Car

After phoning her father,
my mother caught a ride from the depot.
Her kid brother waited at the bridge
and then ran, grinning, beside the car
all the way to the house.
He was taller and bonier than the day she left,
bib overalls hanging on his shirtless shoulders,
thick dark hair shaking with his running.

He clammed up and backed off when she
got out. She held her squirming baby
and stood at the driver's window to thank
the neighbor who had given her a ride,
the long thanks protocol called for.
Neither father nor mother came to the door,
one reading the county paper
and one peeling an extra potato. It was
her kid brother who reached for her suitcase
and ran ahead over the cedar needles
to open the heavy door.

We Visit the Homestead

The old woman shows me the location
where her father, years ago, fell dead
under the trees, beside the buzz saw,
the broken blade in his throat.
Spot of grass where he lay
when she ran from house and saw him.
Will you stay with the body, someone asked her,
and she did. Knelt beside the body,
laid a dish towel over his face.
The body dressed as it was in chore clothes,
layers of shirts, heavy coat. The body,
needing to work, needing cattle,
a horse to ride, a barn to build,
as if work were nourishment:
lift this, carry it, never put it down.
The body, marvelous when bending,
beautiful striding, kneeling, hammering,
exquisite the movement, the dance.
She turns to face me. Her hands
on my shoulders, she tells me:
You can always do—
her lips purse and flex, her teeth are small, gray—
You can always do what you have to do.

One-Finger Wave

A momentary camaraderie, an interstice,
a greeting between wayfarers:

the one-finger wave between ranchers
on the roads through the sandhills of Nebraska.

My car, going north,
meets a cattle truck loaded with Angus, going south.

At the proper moment,
the proper distance,

my hands still on the wheel,
I raise my index finger

and the stranger does the same
as if to say:

In our most solitary orbits
we are sometimes not alone.

From *Lost in Seward
County*, 2001

The Sisters Play Canasta in a Snowstorm

The sister who can drive
picks up the others,
keeping the Pontiac chugging
in each driveway while a sister steps out,

pulling her door shut behind her,
putting on her new Christmas stocking mittens.
We have no business out in such a storm, one says, laughing,
no business at all.

But the wind takes her words and swirls them
like snow across the windshield. It's on to the next house,
the next sister. At the last house they play canasta,
the deuces wild, even as they were in childhood,

the wind blowing through the empty apple trees,
the shadows of bumper crops.
They're kids again, planning a prank in their farmhouse
while a salesman gets out of his car with his briefcase.

Let's drape a sheet over Margaret's head—
Margaret will do it—our ghost
bobbing and moaning in the doorway
in broad daylight. We got rid of that one—
bring on the next one! We're rascals
sure as barnyard dogs—we're wild card players.

The snow thickens, the coffee perks,
and nothing is lost if it can be retold.

We'll have to quit someday, one or the other says.
We are getting up there in the years. We'll have to quit,
but today—
deal, sister, deal!

Overheard at the Cafe

I knew this guy once, went to Europe
supposed to go with three girls
they chickened out so he went by himself
takes a lot of guts
not knowing the language
you take your vacations
some people drive to the Grand Canyon
get out, take their picture in front of their car
they get back
they say: wanna see my pictures?
me, I drive out of the county once in a great while
throw a beer can out of the car
come back, that's my vacation
heard on the radio the average man
dies at the age of 69
the average woman lives to 72
wonder why that is
'course, you take your averages
you stand one leg in a bucket of hot water,
the other in cold,
on an average, you
should be comfortable.
But you're not.

Otto

who stood at the edge of family pictures
the shade of the oak tree
blotching his face
whose hands held his gray felt hat
behind him, rolling the brim
toward the sweat band
whose brown suit grew
season by season too large
each harvest inching farther down
on his wrists toward the large nubs of his knuckles

whose voice caught at the start of his sentence
like a plow settling into a new furrow
who did not sing in church
his very clean hands folded over his knees

who on summer afternoons
poured cold coffee into his white cup
who said he liked it

who owned a bed in his brother's farmhouse
(no flop-ear brown dog running to the gate
ever known as Otto's
no pipe
no International
no bad jokes
no twenty-two
no girl as far as anybody said

no child of his
crying or sleeping on the second floor
in the dark house)
who before reaching up for his hat
on the nail above the separator
would stand
mornings
at the screen door
his hands in his back pockets.

As Long as Someone Remembers

I remember the round shape of the ward,
the nurse's station in the center, the young nurse
Rhonda, a South Dakota girl, soft-hearted.
I remember the blue sweater she wore
over her uniform. The ward was cold. She said
she'd scrounge around for more blankets.
She brought five of them, white cotton
hospital blankets for us, to keep him warm
and also at night for my mother in
the brown chair by the bed. He wasn't eating.
Maybe he had decided Enough is enough,
but then his old buddy Curly came and talked to him.
Curly in the brown chair, talking to
the silent man in the bed.

Rhonda's eyes filled with tears the morning
she knew he wasn't going to make it, but first
there was the morning he decided to eat again.
I was glad, I watched him swallow,
I left the room and let myself smile in the hall,
raised my fist, said *Yes!* I should have gone back in
and said thanks for this too, this one more try,
this pain you are going to stretch out longer for
those of us who come and go in the brown chair.
I was grateful, couldn't say it,
walked a victory lap around the ward, went back in
to see if he wanted to stand at the window
and look out.

Summer, Striking

At just the right time my father struck the mortar,
struck being the proper term for the gentle motion
of smoothing the seams between the blocks,
the mortar set up but not yet hard,
this necessary striking that was not striking at all
and sometimes he let me do the striking,
child hanging around, helping.

He was laying blocks for a building in the country,
he and I the only humans,
nothing nearby but pasture, a road,
a stand of trees, a herd of Angus.

Not much good as helper, I could not
lift the blocks into their places on the wall.
I could fetch the blue chalk line; I could
lug a half-pail of *mud*, his term for mortar.
I was not a true assistant those long days in the sun,
the new wall taking shape course by course,

the birds one by one by one into the trees,
cardinals mostly, and jays,
their morning songs when we began,
their twilight sounds when we called it quits

but it's the noontime I remember, that long
and drowsy hour when we ate the sandwiches and rested.
Stretched out in the grass under the cottonwoods,

his cap over his face, he dozed; I played with pebbles,
made a row of stones, listened to the silence,
watched a jet make a thin white contrail.

This was the time between,
this was the mortar,
and we struck it lightly, gave it shape:
two small figures,
one in the shade, reclining,
one standing in the sun, looking up, shading her eyes,
alone on a shimmering plain.

You Gave Me a Typewriter

You gave me a typewriter for Christmas. Before I
unwrapped the box, I thought it was an accordion. I think

you had asked me which I wanted. I think I didn't know.
I think I said *Either*. I was young, high school,

so much space, as now, between *know* and *don't know*.
I didn't know what was in the package, a present for me,

oldest daughter, nerdy, egghead, interested in music,
no piano in the house, my uncle's accordion heavy when

it hung on my young neck, when I tried to move my wrists
and hands as he had moved his over the array of buttons,

over the white keys and the black. His fingers found
those buttons in their rows, pushed the correct one,

quick and off. His eyes could stay on the sheet music
while he played, while he pulled the instrument open

and pushed it back. "Lady of Spain"
stretched out, lengthened, shook,

and folded up again, the music filling the house.
Perhaps a small accordion for me in the package, my

Christmas present, my gift, special, and I tried
to be glad it was the gray case of a gray typewriter,

a Remington, portable, something I needed.
Did you want an accordion, you asked me.

No, I said. I'll play this.

Lying on the Driveway, Studying Stars

Through the eye of the binoculars
stars are not steady;
they quiver minutely
as muscles in tired arms

and Cassiopeia is taken apart,
each separate star
swimming to you in a small round sky,
bobbing, giddy, before becoming quiet:

a young woman in a distant city
crying.

Holed Up in Valentine, Nebraska

My room on the second floor of the Comfort Inn
looks out on trees flailing their skinny arms.
Wind out of the north 30 to 40, gusting to 50,
the face in the TV says. I can say it blew the sunrise
all the way to gray. The third snowplow since 5:45

grinds by on the highway. Here I am,
holed up in Cherry County: poet-in-the-schools,
schools closed on account of snow,
plenty of leisure and pretzels, plenty of
hours to write a chapbook on anything handy.
Or iron all my socks.

The wind swirls the skirt of snow on the roof of the lumberyard.
A couple of black dogs don't give a darn for blizzard conditions
or total accumulations. They chase each other out of sight.
The ice machine in the hall dumps its paydirt
into its lap as it did all day yesterday.
There's something new here, must be.

There's a waffle machine at the self-serve breakfast downstairs,
and poppy seed muffins. They're pretty good, the nice lady
from Fargo tells me. She's snowed in, too,
on her way to Phoenix. I imagine the Niobrara,

lying low in the drifted banks while this thing blows over.
I imagine a Charolais or an Angus, head down,
turning tail to the wind. Out of the snowbank
at the edge of the parking lot, a single stalk of dry prairie grass
flops like a metronome. Yes, 30 to 40, gusting to 50.
Life blows on.

Prairie Pretends to Be Mild

Prairie trots out her February hoax, her melt down,
her best dress for the blind date. But I'm not blind.

Still, here are her cafes, their doors open to the street.
I'm not throwing my mittens away. She's so

coy, her rivers wearing only a little ice,
the provocative slip showing. Trust me,

Prairie says, I love you. And she does,
her switchgrass lying down with whispers

in a western breeze. Trust me, too, I answer.
Wrap me in grasses, call to me with cranes

and plovers, snow geese, meadowlarks.
Watch me with the quiet lover's eyes

of kingbirds. Hold me, child and woman,
rock me, your wild indigo tangled in my hair.

The Muse Is a Little Girl

The muse is a little girl, impossibly polite.
She arrives when you're talking
or walking away from your car.
She's barefoot, she stands
next to you, mute; she taps your sleeve,
not even on your skin, just touches the cloth
of your plaid shirt, touches it twice
with her index finger
and you keep talking, or you don't.
She will wait one minute. She is not hungry
or unhappy or poor. She goes somewhere else
unless you turn and look at her
and write it down. Or maybe
she's a horse you want to ride, she's a tall horse,
she's heavy, as if she could bear armor.
You can't catch her with apples.
I don't know how to get on.
I remember my cold fingers
grasping the black mane.

Night Flight

From 18F I see only the wing,
see only metal and rivets and painted black arrows
and partially worn-off letters saying things like NO STEP.
From 18F, or anywhere on this plane,
I could see, if I want to, the video.
I could, evidently, watch *Buzz Lightyear*, the series.
But I am watching us, the community
of 1090 to Denver. We are facing forward
as though in a tunnel or tube,
dots of light in a row above our heads.
We are ranks of readers, sleepers.

or we are the cast of *Our Town*;
we are cast as the dear departed,
sitting onstage on our chairs—supposed to be graves—
looking straight ahead, talking among ourselves,
never looking at Emily, the living,
when she comes to visit the cemetery.
We are not turning toward Emily;

we are numbers and letters facing forward.
From 18F I see we are regular in our posture,
regular in our habits.

In my row we are raising similar cups from similar trays,
oddly comforting.
Now this head, now that one, lowers to drink.
One by one we sip our mutual nectar;
one by one we set it down.

From *Bones of a Very Fine Hand*, 1999

Resurrection

After the spring snowstorm
I go out to save trees, shaking them
as if they were sleepers,
hanging on when they lift,
standing in waterfalls of snow,
my hair awash with it,
my earrings cold on my neck.

I crack off a dead limb from the redbud
and use it, a scepter,
on the forsythia: yellow flowers
bloom out of snow. The yews
rise, healed. I get carried away and
go on to someone else's woods to save trees.

I reach into snow, feeling for femur,
for tibia, ulna, radius,
pulling them up, shaking them,
hitting them with my pole,
my face up to snow coming
down, my mouth open to eat,
glasses covered, snow behind the lenses,
wet snatches burning my cheeks where
I brushed against cedars.

I turn back toward the house,
an old man stumbling,
my jacket whitened,
arms hanging as if long branches,
hands numb in my gloves,

a grin on my blind face.
I walk through drifts chanting:

Rise.

Rise.

The Green Coat

It was a good wool and a good cut,
gold-colored buttons heavy and embossed;
shawl collar lying on her straight shoulders.
She came out of the living quarters into
the kitchen in the green coat,

no one in the cafe but her brother
at the counter and her husband talking
to him, these two men having bought
the coat, having brought it to her.
They had been waiting and she coughed
in the way she did when she didn't

know what to say. She unbuttoned
a button, slid her hand into the pocket.
Her husband came into the kitchen,
giving a wolf-whistle. Her hair was
brushed back, her lashes on her cheeks,
her eyes looking at the floor.

Keeping My Mother Warm

I gave a down shirt: rib-knit collar, snaps,
forest green. She said she wears it in the house.
I gave a jacket: royal blue, zipper, hood, premier
northern goose down. When she scrubbed

makeup off the collar, she bleached
the color out but she said she doesn't mind.
I gave a black cotton sweater, a jillion red roses
embroidered on the front, heavy as chain mail,

elastic in the cuffs. She said she washed it,
dried it in the dryer, said it held up
pretty well. I gave a sleek wool blend, gray
with white cables. Perhaps it flaps

on her washline even now. Maybe it tumbles,
cuffs over crewneck, in her dryer.
I should make her a quilt. A quilt
for the quiltmaker. Last night I slept

under a quilt she sewed: gorgeous prairie,
sea of many colors. Red velvet triangles,
yellow satin trapezoids, purple silk
parallelograms, dark shining rhombuses—

her feather stitch holding every crazy thing
together. Thanks, Mom, for that beauty.
May your loneliness go south for the winter.
May your old friends bring you cake. May you

beat them at pitch, pinochle, hearts, and gossip.
May the mail arrive early with gifts. May
hummingbirds remember where all your
windows are. May your feet be warm as

waffles, warm as buckwheat cakes, warm as
sweethearts. May your fingers limber and
flex above any patch you ever want. May all your
pies be chocolate. Love, Me. Love me. Love me. Love me.

Saying Yes on the Road

My husband and I are singing in the car,
passing a red pickup from Indiana that
looks like every pickup we have ever passed.
In the old days when our song came up on the tapes,
the kids in the back were embarrassed,
my husband holding my hand
and singing toward the white lines
in the highway, asking me not to

leave him lonely.
It's a new song today,
our songs like our hands having changed,
softer, not so needy, not so sleek.

By day the lush green corn or dry brown stalks.
At night the bridges and the flat white rivers under the moon,
the lights of cities flung on the dark.

My husband in the front, driving, singing.
And I, in the back, my papers and books
spread around me. He's reaching
over his shoulder to touch my hand,
my hand reaching up to him,
as if the concave of our palms
could get closer to this closeness,
as if we could give *yes* to what comes beyond the rise,
beyond this swell of ground the road follows.

Perfume Counter, Dillard's

The clerk shows him cologne, thinking
that's what he means, a thirty-dollar
plastic spray bottle. No, he says,
his checkbook open flat on the glass
of the counter. No, in his bargain
T-shirt, fifteen-dollar haircut,
Wards jeans. No, he says
softly. Perfume. She brings up

from the depths in their boxes
one-quarter ounce,
one-third ounce,
one-half ounce, and
tells him the price of each,
which he sort of knows from
last time. And I in my five-year-old
Lake Superior many-washed gray

sweatshirt and my hair all over
the place with rain and wind and
the wrong shampoo know
what she doesn't:
he'll take the real thing, the big size
and because I further know if I should be so
foolish as to give up the ghost,
kick the bucket, cash in my chips,
he would—not that he's fickle—eventually buy
some good brand for some other woman,

I make my plan—
the universe being thrown together as it is—to live,
to be the no-substitute,
the real,
the one hanging in there
beside him while he writes the check
and signs it and draws a line
under his name.

The World Was Not Enough

It was Sunday morning, and when I got home
from the prairie, my son had gone to church, so
I put on my jacket and went too. When I entered
the building, I waited to see if I'd get a feel
for which side to go to, which side he was on,
but two women talking loud in the anteroom
ruined my concentration. I went to the
south side and tried to see through the watery glass
in the door, crouching to see if anyone
sat in the blur I thought was the back of a chair.
I opened the door a crack, no usher to stop me
because the service was two-thirds over,
and I saw him

across the room on the other side—
blond, big, intense—how I love that
unplanned child, his generous grin and
the sort of sideways hop he will do, coming to give
me a hug when he sees me in the kitchen in the morning
or when he comes home happy. I saw him, arms crossed,
glasses, saw all in one second, saw the heaviness
of the tweed coat on the warm day,
his face turned to the speaker,
one inch and one second all I needed, but I
looked at him long and enjoyed it, and went

around through the room where
the women were still talking. I went to
the clouded glass of the double doors on that side,
had to look through the crack again.
I sat in the last row with the ushers and
watched the hair on the back of my son's
head and thought about the world,
the world that is not enough for me without him in it.

Loving Her in the Mountains

Hard climb behind us,
we clown around on the tundra,
my daughter and I,
laughing. The sleeves of my
too-big sweater swing limp
beyond my hands. She pushes

the bandana over my eyes.
I dance for her blindfolded, goofy,
the water in the canteen
sloshing with my spinning and
twirling. My daughter laughs
until no sound comes and she
must sit, voiceless, on the rocks
to recover. On this day

in this place,
the peaks standing watch,
I love her and I can only
dance it, my old shoes
quick as the feet of a deer on the grasses.

I Let My Daughter Down

She brings home a cardboard box,
opens the lid, her hands sleek,
moving as if ready to weave
or play a stringed instrument.
She lifts out a chick and gives it
to me. Nobody, she says,
would take this one.

The feet of the chick are
wads of toes. He sits on his
elbows. Something happened,
I say, in the egg. My daughter's eyes
are lovely. Fairness. A chance
for everybody. She names him Pegasus.
We set his box in the basement
bathroom away from the cats.
The dandelion fuzz on Pegasus
goes to pinfeathers. He straddles
bravely, the distance from one
foot to the other widening.

Outside his window: the rains,
the quiet mornings. On the patio
a robin turning over twigs.

See how he eats, she says,
with a will to correct himself.

Neither one of us knows
how I could do such a thing,
but I give the chick away
to someone in the country.
She never looks at me the same again.
And I can't blame her, shod as I am
in these red fandango shoes,
wearing as I must
this gaudy dress, my unfairnesses
flashing like sequins.

Cutting My Hair

Heavy with child, my daughter
kneels behind my chair on newspapers
spread on her kitchen floor. She's
cutting my hair; I'm crying and

mad because I'm making things worse
by crying. I want to stop this haircut.
Half-done is fine with me. I grab her
wrist behind my head, but she pulls away.
We struggle: a pregnant woman on her knees,
and her mother, holding her wrist.
I'm just as stubborn, she says,

and more so. She won't stop cutting
and cutting. I sit with my face in the
towel. She says *It's all right,*
forget it, let me finish this,
let me do what I have to do.
I let her cut my hair, small pieces falling,
shedding onto the flannel shirt
she wears over the baby. Near my ear

the hairs grate against the blade,
steady, slow. Her knees shift
the papers as she circles me.
It's guilt, she says. *I've had it too,*
I've had it plenty.

My face in the towel,
my head at the angle for the haircut,
I can't stop her cutting,

parting, combing,
making me feel better.
When I finish here, she says,
you'll be ready for a hug.

Washing the Walls

My daughter wants the house clean, wants me to
leave my shoes at the door. She's nesting,
large and tired, awaiting the child. This is a way

I love her: I'm on a ladder
washing the walls, washing windows,
my hand over the ledges and sills
and floors of her house,
my hand across glass
corner to corner to corner.

Tonight she rests in a chair and reads to me
comics and editorials while I dust the blinds.
I laugh and I clean. Another joke, another slat.
We talk about the time I was pregnant with her.
She wants to know these things,
how she fits in, how her child fits in;
she is fierce to prepare the bed
and the clothes for him,
the books and music. Now she
sits before her shelves
and shows me what she has,
what is ready. Once before sunrise

she pulled her luggage down the streets
of Oxford to the Green line bus stop.

After cold cereal at the landlady's,
the sound of the wheels of her suitcase
on the sidewalk to the bus and then the plane.
All that day in my mind
I watched the winter storms, her path unlit
until it opened like a fallopian tube to a place
where I waited to gather her, safe and home,

waited as now she waits. She touches her belly,
her fingers circling, keeping the searchlight on,
sweeping the dark. It's her child. Nobody
will love him as she does, watching his progress
over the pole, the strong winds at the higher
elevations, the crackpots in the airports
with guns and explosives and axes to grind,
nobody assigned to the child as she is assigned.

My gift: these moist surfaces,
the shine of the wood,
the peppermint soap in the rag,
my hand moving

along the baseboards,
drawing boundaries,
my hand washing the walls,
this for the love of her

who lay in the dark of my body
as now, still, the thought of her
lies light and steady where
hope is, where it stays, where it lives.

Taking the Baby to the Marsh

We walk the wetland,
our weight lowering the pontoon boardwalk,
my daughter carrying her son, telling him

about the marshgrass, telling him where he is.
He is in her arms; she is wrapping the blue blanket
around him, pulling his cap to cover his ear.
I want to remember how she holds her son,

turns him to see the Canada goose walking,
the goose laying his flat hands down again and again
on the boards. Now the baby watches,
his face all interest for the takeoff,

the honking, the wings grazing air.
It's my turn; I take the child,
pull the wings of my coat around him.
As he is falling asleep I whisper

into his soft new ear. I say: *red twig, black water.*
I say *king goose, queen hawk.*
I say *grass.*
I say *wind.*
I say *mother.*

Shopping

I would buy for my daughter earrings
of pale green and indigo glass.
She would think them odd, would love them,
would say, What were you thinking?

In my mind I lay them into a carved red box,
the pads of my fingers over
the circles and petals on the lid.
I would be colorful and generous,

the fine lines in her throat, the shine
of her eyes. I buy a barrette
for the braid that sometimes lies
above the bones of her shoulders,
on the right or the left when she turns.
A bauble, the light shining on it,
a yellow floating up inside the brown

under the surface. I want her hands
to open the clasp, her elbows in the air,
my daughter talking to someone as
she fastens it, or talking to no one
but herself in front of the mirror
in the morning. I want to have given,

to have wrapped in blue paper
crackling and wrinkling like
years of not going wild, of
sensible conservation.
She may think sometimes how I gave her
this or that. She will wear it, this modest pin,
this abundant love, her rich dark hair.

Storm at Night

About one in the morning on Indian Island
the wind wakes me, sucking in the sides of the tent.
The lightning so bright that after it is gone,
it remains on the backs of my eyelids.
On the backs of my eyelids the hoops and zippers
of the inside of the tent. Thunder close
and huge over me. Rain beating
on the purple poppy mallow, as I imagine it,
low against the ground in the dark.

The surface of the Platte, as I imagine it,
peppered as if with stones,
I am thinking of my friend who,
when he knew he was going to die,
sat in his yard in the sunshine
with his neighbor. The two of them
on blue lawn chairs, drinking Stroh's.
Rolling cigarettes, making a trough with
the index finger in squares of white paper,
shaking tobacco into the trough, rolling,
licking the papers, trying again.
Neither of them smokers, smoking.
Not talking about illness.

The Platte from its source
around and over gray boulders, flowing
beside Indian Island, beneath thunder,
white for a moment under lightning,
its broad surface wrinkling like skin.

I am thinking of Crazy Horse, who
before he died, asked for the man who had
pushed the bayonet into the soft parts of his back.
Asked for that one to stand before him, and spoke
to him of pardon. Crazy Horse in his
bloody graveclothes. His mother and father
receiving the body of their child
to put into the cart.

A wind high in the cottonwoods,
the crickets stroking the dark.
After rain, not sleeping, thinking
of my daughter who called
to say she cut her hand with a
knife in her kitchen. My daughter
far down the flow of the Platte,
learning of my grandmother's remedy,
using her poultice of sugar and alcohol.
The cut, as I imagine it, healing.
My daughter's brown hair,
as I imagine it, hanging above

their hands. Young woman's hands,
old woman's hands
laying the white poultice
against the red line of the scab,
winding strips of cloth,
wrapping the wound.
The Platte from its source
peppered by night rains.
In the morning the river will sparkle
like leaves turning in wind.
The Platte flowing over its sand bars,
around the smooth white bones
of its cottonwood logs.

I Want to Create

I want to create, bring forth,
to say *Let there be*. To make a heron
rise off the pond, tucking his neck
into the shape I want to give it,
flapping his wings enough to clear
the cedars, to clear me, want to
create my grandmother looking
in the weeds for the money I dropped,
nickels and dimes and pennies
in the knot in the corner of
the lavender hanky, to look for it
at the base of the ragweed stems
as if she were searching for me,
as if she could find what is lost,
her back rounded, bent over,
the buttons of the thin summer dress,
her stockings in the hot sun,
her hair coming out of the roll,
looking for what cannot be found.
I want someone to believe the heron,
believe the spine, the woman bending,
the coins missing, believe she forgave me,
came out to the overgrown field and looked
for it, the impossible loss,
the sun beating down on us,
the shade of blue over the wings and back,
the liftoff from a prairie pond,
someone to believe the air over the water,

the flapping, I want someone—
I want to be the one—to stand up,
holding the lost—rediscovered and powerful—
in the palm of the hand, to say with
amazement: *Look, I found it.*

The Last Thing He Said

The last thing he said was *Yes*.
Maybe he was answering my mother's
question, maybe it was mine. I wanted
to be sure he had enough morphine, enough
of anything he wanted. It had shrunk
to one room. One breath at a time
pulled like knotted twine
in and out through a hole in a board.
Louie, can you hear
Sometimes I rise and roam the house
a woman with fears, window to window.
Louie, can you hear me
Are you in pain
For no good reason—
parallelograms of moonshine
on the cool dark floors—
I am beginning to feel better,
a woman with fears
a woman with love.
Frost on the shingles
oak trees
grass.

Today

Today on the anniversary of my father's death
I walked on the dam among the geese,
the whole flock quiet as they are sometimes
when you walk through them at sunrise,
then one shaking out her wings
and running toward a direction,
the others in the air with her

before you can figure out who is truly the leader.
It was twelve years ago today, giving as little trouble
as he could, dying on a Sunday
in the daytime, not thrashing about.
The geese lift off, folding their legs back as if
that's the way they prefer it,

slipping into air, their toes pointed behind them.
He had smiled in photographs,
happy to stand beside his beloved,
the space ready, the year of birth

cut into granite, numbers already there,
curves in speckled polished stone.
Today there are old songs on the radio
and we sing along together in the car,
my husband and I, two fools

singing down 27th Street, weaving in and out,
sitting in the line backed up at the light,

and we don't care
if we look ridiculous, singing
and jabbing each other. The light's green
and there's another song coming.

To order or obtain more information on these or other University of Nebraska Press titles, visit nebraskapress.unl.edu.

Lightning Source UK Ltd.
Milton Keynes UK
UKHW011358290821
389562UK00011B/493